ROADSIDE MEMORIES

A Collection of Vintage Gas Station Photographs

Todd P. Helms & Chip Flohe

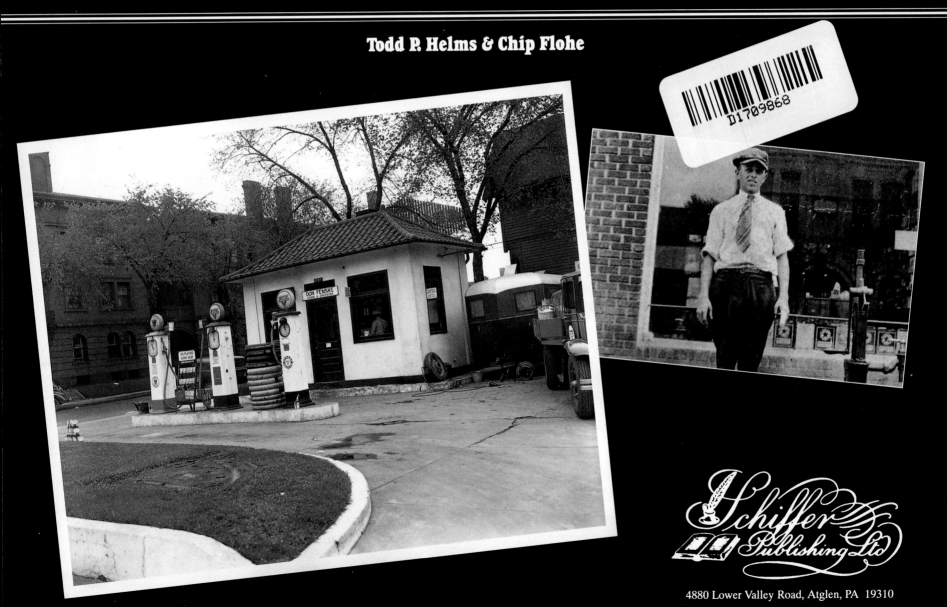

Schiffer Publishing Ltd

4880 Lower Valley Road, Atglen, PA 19310

This book is dedicated to the memory of the "service" station, a perfect example of what's missing in today's fast-paced world.

Published by Schiffer Publishing Ltd.
4880 Lower Valley Road
Atglen, PA 19310
Phone: (610) 593-1777; Fax: (610) 593-2002
E-Mail: Schifferbk@aol.com
Please write for a free catalog.
This book may be purchased from the publisher.
Please include $2.95 for shipping.
Try your bookstore first.

We are interested in hearing from authors
with book ideas on related subjects.

TABLE OF CONTENTS

ACKNOWLEDGMENTS

The authors wish to thank a large group of people and/or organizations for their contributions to this book. They are: John Simmons, Jack Keathly, Vic Hannan, John Beltz, Minnesota Historical Society, Jim DuRose, Conoco, Inc., Fairfield County Public Library, Harr's Service Station, Lou Schaffer, Steven Sullivan, James Woodard, Englewood BP, Bob Peterson, Craig Cruise, Jeff Stooksbury, Max Denton, and Sam Jett.

Copies of the photos in this book are available by contacting:

Chip Flohe
3950 Newport Highway
Sevierville, TN 37876
(423)453-8026

Todd Helms
1023 East 5th Ave.
Lancaster, OH 43130
(614)654-6179

INTRODUCTION

In this book, we are offering a glimpse into our not-so-distant past. If you're lucky, you still might find the shell of one of these old service stations on a forgotten back road or on the back streets of some small town. With their roofs caved in and grass growing window high, these buildings are usually not even noticed by most passerbys, and if they are, they are considered an eyesore. To us, this is the spark that ignites memories of a time when life was slower paced and a little less complicated. In those days, 10 cents would buy a Coke *and* a candy bar, men would gather at the neighborhood station on Saturday mornings to sit and tell tall tales, and service station attendants would fall all over themselves to meet your every need. Today, it's not uncommon to pull into a convenience store, pay at the pump with your credit card, and never even talk to a human being. And this is progress?

This book is meant to aid and delight collectors, historians, and anyone who loves Americana. Nothing personifies our love affair with the automobile and travel in America more than the service stations that sprang up beginning in the early 1900s.

Our book is organized with a chapter dedicated to each individual company or group of companies, allowing the reader to concentrate his/her attention on a particular company of interest. Chapter 1 gives a broad overview of the history behind the gasoline service station and how it has evolved into the "convenience" store of the 90s.

At the beginning of each chapter is a brief history of the company featured. Our intent, however, was not to go into great detail in this area. Several very good books are already on the market to address this subject (see the Suggested Reading section for more information). Our goal is to give the reader a broad-brushed glimpse into the past with hundreds of hard to find photos of the stations which once populated our countryside.

Now, come with us for a walk down memory lane!

There are several things in life that are difficult to pinpoint as being the first of their kind, and service stations are no exception. Many companies lay claim to having the first service station in the United States. As we move through the history of service stations in this chapter, we will explore some of these self-proclaimed pioneers.

The roots of the modern day service station began back in the late 1800s when farmers and merchants began using fuel oil for heat and light. At that time, petroleum products could be purchased at bulk plants, general stores, or delivered by tank wagon.

With the advent of the gasoline powered automobile by German scientists Benz and Daimler in 1875, a demand developed for a new petroleum product. It wasn't until Frank and Charles Duryea built the first American made gasoline powered automobile in 1892 and Henry Ford introduced mass produced automobiles in the United States in 1903 that there became a need for more centrally located and specialized vendors.

By mass producing cars, Ford was able to make affordable what was once a novelty for only the rich to enjoy. Therein began this nation's love affair with the car. With its rising popularity came the development of gasoline retailing followed closely by name brand marketing. By 1912, there were more than a half million vehicles on America's crude highway system.

Of those claiming to have the "first" service station, Standard Oil of California (now Chevron), probably has the legitimate claim to the throne. In 1907, Standard built the first U.S. service station near its Seattle kerosene refinery. This "station" consisted of a shed, a 30 gallon tank, and a garden hose. It drew up to 200 customers a day.

Several years later, in 1909, a Shell agent near St. Louis, built the first "drive-in" station to be separated from a bulk plant. This station was also nothing more than a shed covering barrels of oil and two converted hot-water tanks containing gasoline with a garden hose dispensing system.

Soon to follow was the first building built exclusively for gasoline distribution in 1910 by Central Oil Company of Flint, Michigan, and then the first architect-designed station by Gulf in Pittsburgh in 1913. From these early roots, the gas station of the 1920s-1970s was born.

Oddly enough, this booming new American business was predominately controlled early on by one giant corporation, Standard Oil. Standard Oil was created by John D. Rockefeller and his associates in 1863 in Cleveland, Ohio. Around 1900, Standard Oil consisted of about twenty different companies, produced about thirty-three percent of America's crude, and refined about eighty percent of the finished product. If this seems a little one-sided, you're right. In 1911, the Standard Oil Trust was dissolved by the Supreme Court into thirty-

Sinclair Station, Chapman Highway, Knoxville, Tennessee. Circa 1940s.

Between brands. Chapman Highway, Knoxville, Tennessee. Circa 1950s.

four separate companies. Many of today's major oil companies were born out of the ruins of this break up (i.e. Exxon, Arco, Conoco, Amoco, Chevron, etc.). In the chapters to follow, we will give a brief history of the companies featured, how and when they began, and where they marketed.

After the Standard Oil demise, the service station industry boomed. More than 200 new petroleum companies were formed in 1916 alone. By 1920, there were more than 15,000 gas stations in America. Until this time, however, customers still had to pump their own fuel. Beginning in the early 1920s, the era of "Full" service began. It was around this time that the tall, glass-domed "visible" gas pumps appeared and station attendants began pumping gas, cleaning windshields, and checking the oil, water, and tires.

In the 1930s, the gas station became an integral part of the landscape and our lives. By 1933, there were over 24 million registered automobiles in the United States. Stations became more complicated and sophisticated in design. Some retailers went to extremes in their design to attract customers. Buildings were built to resemble airplanes, gas pumps, tea pots, etc. Stations also began to offer a variety of merchan-

dise other than oil and gas. Items such as tires, batteries, belts, and wiper blades began appearing. It was also during this time that the gas company credit card was born.

The 1940s saw the evolution of the gas station to a more modern design and functionality. Tall, sleek electric pumps replaced the glass visible pumps of the 1920s and 30s. It was also during the 1940s that brand name recognition became important for retailers. Attempts were made by retailers through merchandising and services to entice customer loyalty.

The 1950s and 60s were the heyday for the full-service gasoline service station. The post-war era saw a huge demand by Americans for cars and gasoline as well as every other consumer product imaginable. It was also during this time that the highway system in the U.S. began improving dramatically. With the improved highways came the desire to travel and see America. "Freebies" became the trick of the trade for gasoline marketing. Customers were given free road maps, drinking glasses, trading stamps, china, toys, etc. Sinclair's "Dino", Texaco's fire chief hat, and similar toys became the want of every boy and girl traveling on the road.

Location unknown. Circa 1920s.

7th Avenue, Memphis, Tennessee. Circa 1940s.

Station from pg.5, re-branded as Gulf. Chapman Highway, Knoxville, Tennessee. Circa 1950s.

Crossville, Tennessee. Circa 1940s.

Charleston, South Carolina.
Circa 1950s.

Shreveport, Louisiana.
Circa 1930s.

In the 1970s, gasoline marketing strategies took a decisive turn in their focus. The fuel shortage which plagued the world in the late 1970s and the lines of cars that developed, forced retailers to turn their attention toward ways of saving their customers time and money. As a result, self-serve pumps re-emerged. In 1974, only 6 percent of stations allowed their customers to pump their own fuel. By 1978, this number had grown to 68 percent.

It was also during this era that service bays began to disappear. Cars were being built better, had longer warranties, and became more difficult to repair. To help fill this void, stations began closing in their service bays and the "convenience" store was born. Customers could now buy bread, milk, and other needs after they had pumped their own gas.

The gas station had now gone full circle. In the beginning, general stores that sold food just happened to sell fuel oil. Now, stations that sell gas, just happen to sell food. Today, their are nearly 200 million vehicles on the road with about 210,000 gasoline retailers nationwide. With those figures, it's hard for anyone to argue that the stations pictured on the pages to follow are just a forgotten memory. These are the key to the past and to the future. We hope you enjoy!

Cairo, Georgia. Circa 1950s.

As part of the Standard Oil Trust dissolution in 1911, Standard Oil of Indiana was one of eleven companies given the right to use the Standard Oil name. Standard Oil of Indiana marketed under several names in the different states in which they sold gasoline. These names included Standard, American, Amoco, Pan American (Pan-Am), Utoco (Utah Oil Refining Company), and Vico.

Standard Oil of Indiana owes its beginnings to Standard Oil employee Louis Blaustein. In 1910, Mr. Blaustein invested his life savings into a tank wagon kerosene and gasoline business in Baltimore, Maryland. In 1915, he developed a new anti-knock gasoline called Amoco.

Standard Oil of Indiana took control of the Pan American Petroleum and Transport Company (Pan-Am) in 1929. At the time, Pan-Am had 50 percent control of the American Oil Company of Baltimore. They later purchased Standard Oil of Nebraska and the Utah Oil Refining Company.

Over the years, many brands of gasoline were sold under the different company logos of Amoco. Standard Oil sold its famous Red Crown and White Crown gasoline at its stations in the Midwest and Western US. American Oil sold gas under the American logo in the Eastern U.S. and Texas. Early on, Pan-Am sold the Panamoc and Panolene gasoline brands in the South. In the far Western US, Utoco and Vico were the operating arm of Amoco.

Today, Amoco is a world-wide corporation which has diversified into many areas of petroleum related industries (plastic, Styrofoam, etc.). They still sell gasoline products heavily in the North Central, Eastern, and Southern states (particularly Tennessee, Georgia, and Florida).

Bluff City Highway near Bristol, Tennessee. June 1959.

Fort Henry Drive, Kingsport, Tennessee. March 1961.

Bluff City Highway near Bristol, Tennessee. June 1959.

Oak Ridge Turnpike near Knoxville, Tennessee. Circa 1960s.

Knoxville, Tennessee. Circa 1950s.

Hindman Ferry Road, Memphis, Tennessee. Circa 1950s.

Knoxville, Tennessee. Circa 1950s.

Holston Drive, Knoxville, Tennessee. Circa 1950s.

Memphis, Tennessee. September 1954.

Church Hill, Tennessee. Circa 1950s.

Greeneville, Tennessee. Circa 1960s.

Left:
Memphis, Tennessee. July 1954.

Somewhere in Tennessee. Circa 1960s.

Broadway, Knoxville, Tennessee. March 1966.

Kingston, Tennessee. Circa 1960s.

Memphis, Tennessee. May 1965.

Erwin, Tennessee. Circa 1960s.

Near Erwin, Tennessee. Circa 1960s.

Gallatin, Tennessee. Circa 1960s.

Winchester, Tennessee. September 1964.

Kingston Pike, Knoxville, Tennessee. May 1964.

Knoxville, Tennessee. December 1964.

Broadway, Knoxville, Tennessee. March 1966.

Memphis, Tennessee. Circa 1960s.

Highway 441, Sevierville,
Tennessee. Circa 1965.

Location unknown. April 1972.

Lincoln & Peterson, Chicago, Illinois. Circa 1960s.

Highway 126, Blountville, Tennessee. Circa 1930s.

As another member of the Standard Oil Trust dissolution, Standard of New Jersey escaped the break up as the world's largest oil company. After the break up, they maintained some 43 percent of the trust's assets. In the beginning, Standard of New Jersey had a presence in six states: New Jersey, Maryland, Virginia, West Virginia, North Carolina, and South Carolina.

Although Standard of New Jersey purchased many companies through the years, by the 1960s, they only marketed gasoline under six brand names. These brands were Esso, Humble, Carter, Oklahoma, Pate, and Enco. Each brand was very territorial in nature.

Esso stations could be found along the east coast from Maine as far south as South Carolina as well as Louisiana and Arkansas. They sold under the Humble brand in Ohio, Texas, New Mexico, and Arizona. Carter stations were located in the Northwest (Oregon, Washington, Idaho, Montana, Wyoming, Utah, Colorado, North/South Dakota, and Nebraska). Oklahoma, Pate, and Enco were located in Michigan, Illinois, Indiana, and Kentucky.

The Oklahoma, Pate, Carter, and Humble brands were replaced by the Enco brand in 1960-61. Because Standard of New Jersey was prevented from taking its original Esso logo nationwide, it hoped the Esso and Enco names

Somewhere in Middle Tennessee. Circa 1940s.

Oak Ridge Highway, Knoxville, Tennessee. Circa 1940s.

Location unknown. Circa 1940s.

Chapman Highway, Knoxville, Tennessee. Circa 1940s.

Somewhere in Central Tennessee. Circa 1940s.

were similar enough in nature to use in common nationwide advertising. Not creating the market stir they had hoped with the Enco brand, Standard Oil of New Jersey took an unprecedented step in 1971. The Exxon brand name was adopted for the company's U.S. operations. The Esso name was kept everywhere else in the world. Today, Exxon has almost 12,000 outlets in forty states.

Yet another of the original Standard companies, Standard Oil of Kentucky was also born out of the 1911 break-up. Standard Oil of Kentucky, known as

Kyso, was assigned marketing rights to Kentucky, Florida, Georgia, Alabama, and Mississippi. Unlike most other oil companies, Kyso was purely a marketer. They had no production, refineries, pipelines, etc. Standard Oil of New Jersey supplied Kyso with product until 1961. Kyso marketed this product under the Crown and Crown Extra brand names in their 8,700 outlets.

In 1961, Standard Oil of California (Chevron) bought Kyso. Kyso stations kept the Standard name until 1977 when they were re-branded to Chevron.

Chapman Highway, Knoxville, Tennessee. Circa 1940s.

Somewhere in Tennessee. Circa 1940s.

Memphis, Tennessee. Circa 1940s.

Knoxville, Tennessee. Circa 1950s.

Memphis, Tennessee. Circa 1950s.

North Parkway,
Memphis,
Tennessee.
March 1956.

Kingsport, Tennessee. Circa 1950s.

Kingsport, Tennessee. Circa 1950s.

Knoxville, Tennessee. Circa 1950s.

Memphis, Tennessee. October 1956.

Lamar Avenue, Memphis, Tennessee. September 1954.

Memphis, Tennessee. Circa 1950s.

Morristown, Tennessee.
Circa 1950s.

Somewhere in Tennessee. Circa 1950s.

U.S. Highways 64 & 41A, Winchester, Tennessee. Circa 1950s.

Memphis, Tennessee. Circa 1950s.

Memphis, Tennessee. March 1956.

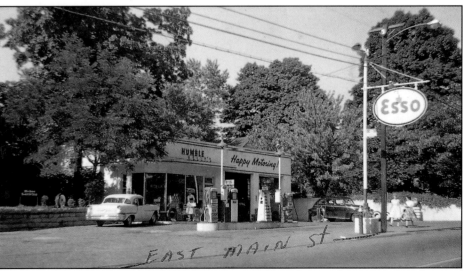

East Main Street, Winchester, Tennessee. Circa 1950s.

Left:
Sevier Avenue,
Knoxville, Tennessee.
Circa 1950s.

Far Left:
Memphis, Tennessee.
Circa 1950s.

Left:
Memphis, Tennessee.
December 1956.

Far Left:
Summer Avenue,
Memphis, Tennessee.
Circa 1950s.

Poplar Avenue, Memphis,
Tennessee. March 1956.

Memphis, Tennessee. July 1957.

Memphis, Tennessee. September 1957.

Milligan College, Johnson City, Tennessee. Circa 1950s.

Bristol, Tennessee. Circa 1950s.

Kingsport, Tennessee. September 1962.

Kingsport, Tennessee. September 1962.

Kingsport, Tennessee. September 1962.

Kingsport, Tennessee. September 1962.

Kingsport, Tennessee. September 1962.

Kingsport, Tennessee. September 1962.

Kingsport, Tennessee. September 1962.

Kingsport, Tennessee. September 1962.

Oak Ridge Highway, Knoxville, Tennessee. Circa 1950s.

Fort Henry Drive, Kingsport, Tennessee. March 1961.

Knoxville, Tennessee. Circa 1950s.

Memphis, Tennessee. Circa 1960s.

Broadway, Knoxville, Tennessee. October 1965.

Memphis, Tennessee. Circa 1960s.

3rd & Madison, Clarksville, Tennessee. Circa 1950s.

Crossville, Tennessee. Circa 1940s.

Summer Avenue, Memphis, Tennessee. Circa 1960s.

Church Hill, Tennessee. Circa 1954.

Kingsport, Tennessee. Circa 1950s.

Memphis, Tennessee. May 1965.

Memphis, Tennessee. Circa 1960s.

Memphis, Tennessee. Circa 1960s.

Somewhere in Tennessee. May 1961.

Somewhere in Tennessee. October 1961.

Bellevue Blvd., Memphis, Tennessee. Circa 1960s.

Summer & Holmes, Memphis, Tennessee. Circa 1960s.

Poplar Avenue, Memphis, Tennessee. Circa 1960s.

Kingsport, Tennessee. Circa 1940s.

East Center Street, Kingsport, Tennessee. Circa 1950s.

Kyso Station. Louisville, Kentucky. Circa 1960s.

Love Street, Erwin, Tennessee. Circa 1950s.

Knoxville, Tennessee. December 1964.

Fountain City, Tennessee. October 1965.

Mississippi Blvd., Memphis, Tennessee. December 1956.

Knoxville, Tennessee. Circa 1960s.

Morristown,
Tennessee.
Circa 1950s.

Unicoi, Tennessee. Circa 1950s.

Fort Henry, Tennessee. March 1961.

The Continental Oil company began in Ogden, Utah, in 1875. In 1885, it too became an operating unit of Standard Oil. After the 1911 breakup of Standard, Conoco was given rights to six Western states: Idaho, Montana, Wyoming, Colorado, Utah, and New Mexico.

Marland Oil Company was founded in Ponca City, Oklahoma in the early 1910s by E.W. Marland. By 1922, there were stations in eleven states selling under the Marland triangle.

In 1929, New York banker J.P. Morgan arranged a merger between Conoco and Marland. Morgan and his investors had large holdings in both companies and hoped the merger would benefit both companies (and their investment). As a result of the merger, the Conoco name was kept and was used with the Marland triangle to form the Conoco triangle logo used from

Conoco triangle logo used from 1929 through 1974 for brand identification.

Like so many other oil companies of the time, Conoco grew by expansion and the purchase of other regional companies. During the 1950s, Conoco bought Western Oil of Minneapolis, F.P. Kendall and Company (Kayo) of Chattanooga, and Douglas Oil Company of Los Angeles.

One of Conoco's most famous advertising campaigns was their "Hottest Brand Going" campaign of the early 1960s. This campaign emphasized their strong roots to the West and featured a branding iron with the Conoco triangle logo.

Conoco was purchased by DuPont in 1981. Today, Conoco has expanded its marketing territory to include the majority of the continental states.

Going up or coming down?
Location and date unknown.

Hannibal, Missouri. Circa 1927.

Location unknown. Circa 1928.

Marland Barrelling Plant, Ponca City, Oklahoma. Circa 1928.

Marland Delivery Truck. Circa 1928.

Pueblo, Colorado. Circa 1930s.

Pueblo, Colorado. Circa 1930s.

Pueblo, Colorado. Circa 1930s.

Location unknown. Circa 1930s.

Pueblo, Colorado. Circa 1930s.

Pueblo, Colorado. Circa 1930s.

Pueblo, Colorado. Circa 1930s.

Pueblo, Colorado. Circa 1930s.

Pueblo, Colorado. Circa 1930s.

Pueblo, Colorado. Circa 1930s.

Pueblo, Colorado. Circa 1930s.

LaSalle Avenue, Minneapolis, Minnesota. May 1938
(*Minneapolis Star-Journal*, Minnesota Historical Society).

Across from Conoco offices, Ponca City, Oklahoma. Circa 1930s.

Pine & Grand, Ponca City, Oklahoma. Circa 1930s.

Across from Conoco offices, South Avenue, Ponca City, Oklahoma. Circa 1930s.

4th & Grand, Ponca City, Oklahoma. Circa 1930s.

Left:
Ponca City, Oklahoma.
Circa 1930s.

Far Left:
4th & Grand, Ponca City,
Oklahoma. Circa 1930s.

Bottom Left:
Somewhere in Oklahoma.
Circa 1932 (Conoco
Archives).

Bottom Right:
Somewhere in Oklahoma.
Circa 1932 (Conoco
Archives).

Across from Conoco Offices, Ponca City, Oklahoma. Circa 1930s (Conoco Archives).

Across from Conoco Offices, Ponca City, Oklahoma. Circa 1930s (Conoco Archives).

Left:
Moran Ranch, near Bandera, Texas. Circa 1930s (Conoco Archives).

Bottom Left:
Location unknown. Circa 1930s (Conoco Archives).

Bottom Right:
Location unknown. Circa 1930s (Conoco Archives).

Location unknown. Circa 1930s (Conoco Archives).

Location unknown. Circa 1930s (Conoco Archives).

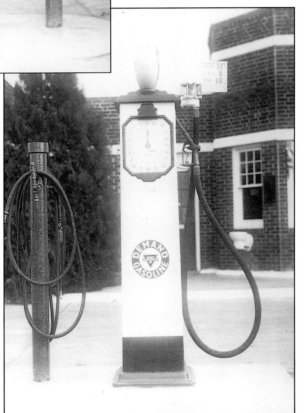

Location unknown. Circa 1930s (Conoco Archives).

Location unknown. Circa 1930s (Conoco Archives).

Night Scene. 4th & Grand,
Ponca City, Oklahoma.
Circa 1930s.

Location unknown. Circa 1930s.

Location unknown. Circa 1930s.

Somewhere in Oklahoma. Circa 1938 (Conoco Archives).

Somewhere in Oklahoma. Circa 1938 (Conoco Archives).

Corpus Christi, Texas. Circa 1934 (Conoco Archives).

Location unknown. Circa 1938 (Conoco Archives).

Location unknown.
Circa 1930s (Conoco
Archives).

Location unknown.
Circa 1930s (Conoco
Archives).

Location unknown. Circa 1930s
(Conoco Archives).

Somewhere in Oklahoma. Circa 1938 (Conoco Archives).

Somewhere in Oklahoma. Circa 1938 (Conoco Archives).

Location unknown. Circa 1938 (Conoco Archives).

Location unknown. Circa 1938 (Conoco Archives).

Top:
Conoco Tank Truck and Merchandising
Bus. Circa 1930s (Conoco Archives).

Below Left:
Conoco Tank Truck. Circa 1930s
(Conoco Archives).

Below Right:
Conoco Tank Truck. Circa 1930s
(Conoco Archives).

Bottom left:
Interior of Merchandising Bus
(Conoco Archives).

Bottom Right:
Interior of Merchandising Bus
(Conoco Archives).

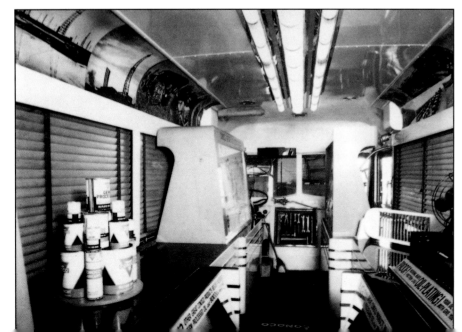

Somewhere in Mississippi. Circa 1950s.

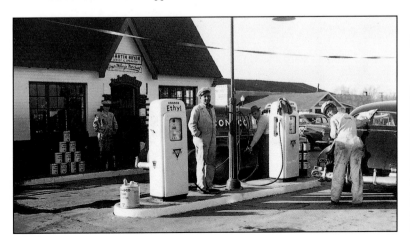

Somewhere in Missouri. Circa 1950s.

Somewhere in Missouri. Circa 1950s.

Maryville, Missouri. Circa 1950.

Lyons, Nebraska. Circa 1950s.

Somewhere in Missouri. Circa 1950s.

Somewhere in Missouri. Circa 1950s.

Somewhere in Missouri. Circa 1950s.

Location unknown. Circa 1950s.

Somewhere in Missouri. Circa 1950s.

Location unknown. Circa 1950s.

Somewhere in Missouri. Circa 1950s.

Location unknown. Circa 1950s.

Location unknown. Circa 1950s.

Location unknown. Circa 1950s.

Kayo Station, Bristol, Tennessee. Circa 1957.

Cities Service began in 1910 as a public service company that provided natural gas and other utility services to its customers in several northeastern metropolitan areas. Soon thereafter, they entered into the petroleum refining and marketing end of the business. Through the 1950s, Cities Service stations were scattered throughout the Northeast, Midwest, and Southwest states.

In the mid 1960s, all of the various Cities Service companies combined to form Citgo. In the late 1960s, Citgo sold rights to their Midwestern stations to Gulf and to their Western Pennsylvania stations to Boron (Standard of Ohio). In 1986, 50 percent of Citgo was sold to the Venezuelan government. Contrary to early image problems, today Citgo claims to have more U.S. retail outlets than anyone else (over 14,000).

Mobil Oil Corporation was born out of Standard Oil of New York (Socony) and its affiliates as a result of the 1911 breakup of the Standard Oil Trust. Socony inherited New York and the New England states in the breakup. In the beginning, Socony specialized in exporting kerosene and selling kerosene and gasoline to non-Socony jobbers. When other brands began invading their territory (Atlantic, Jersey Standard, etc.), Socony established their own branded stations.

Over the next few years, Socony acquired other regional companies. Included in these acquisitions were Magnolia (Texas, Louisiana, Arkansas, Oklahoma, and New Mexico), General Petroleum Company (West Coast and Alaska), White Eagle Oil Company (western states), White Star Refining Company (Michigan), Wadhams Oil Company (Wisconsin), and Lubrite Refining Company (Indiana, Illinois, and Missouri). Several of these companies came to Socony through the Vacuum Oil Company and their merger with Socony in 1931.

Chapman Highway, Knoxville, Tennessee. Circa 1940s.

Erwin, Tennessee. Circa 1940s.

Location unknown. Circa 1950s.

Erwin, Tennessee. Circa 1940s.

Erwin, Tennessee. Circa 1940s.

Vacuum Oil had been Standard Oil's leading exporter of premium lubricating oils. Vacuum held the patents on the Gargoyle and Pegasus trademarks as well as the Mobiloil and Mobilgas brand names. The newly combined company had over 37,000 branded outlets in twenty-nine states.

Through the years, the company went through several name changes: Socony-Mobil, Mobil, and finally the Mobil Corporation in 1966. Today, Mobil markets in thirty states (down from forty-two in 1960). The heart of the Mobil territory remains in New York and the Northeastern states.

Phillips was founded in 1917 in Bartlesville, Oklahoma. Initially a producer of crude oil, Phillips began to refine and market gasoline in 1927. Phillips concentrated on the mid-continent market until 1953 when they purchased their first stations in Florida and began their aggressive marketing expansion. When they bought the West Coast's Flying A from Tidewater in 1966 and opened a single station in Alaska, Phillips became only the second company in history to have branded stations operating in all fifty states at one time. The U.S. District Court later voided the purchase

Location unknown. Circa 1950s.

of Flying A based on antitrust laws. Today, Phillips retails in twenty-nine states with over 7,900 branded stations concentrated in the mid-continent and Southeastern states.

The Sun Oil Company was organized in Ohio in 1890 by the Pew family. Sun began their operations as a producer and a refiner. Their first gas station was built in 1920. By 1928, there were over 500 Sunoco stations in New York, Michigan, Ohio, and Pennsylvania. This number grew to over 9,000 outlets by 1940.

Sun's claim to fame was a premium gasoline called Blue Sunoco. This was a high octane gas which did not contain lead. In the 1950s, Sun introduced custom blending at the pumps. Custom blending gave customers a variety of gasoline grades to choose from.

In 1972, Sun purchased Sunray Mid-Continent. Sunray had over 6,000 branded DX stations located in the Midwest. The result was over 15,000 retail outlets in thirty-four states. In the late 1980s, Sun began a re-imaging campaign and started converting all DX stations to Sunoco. In 1990, Sun had over 6,000 branded stations in twenty-eight states.

Roan Street, Johnson City, Tennessee. Circa 1950s.

Main Street, Jonesboro, Tennessee. Circa 1950s.

Henley Street, Knoxville, Tennessee. Circa 1959.

Henley Street, Knoxville, Tennessee. November 1963.

Broadway, Knoxville, Tennessee. March 1966.

Ernest Flohe's Mobil Station (Chip Flohe's Grandfather),
Briarcliff, New York. Circa 1948.

Turner Filling
Station, South
Columbus Street,
Lancaster, Ohio.
Circa 1933.

Center Street, Kingsport, Tennessee. Circa 1940s.

Location unknown. Circa 1950s.

Memphis, Tennessee. August 1956.

Harris Mobilgas, Memphis, Tennessee. Circa 1950s.

Pennsylvania Avenue, Memphis, Tennessee. Circa 1950s.

Location unknown. Circa 1960s.

Thomas Street, Memphis, Tennessee. Circa 1950s.

Memphis, Tennessee. Circa 1950s.

Memphis, Tennessee. Circa 1960s.

Watauga & Oakland, Elizabethton, Tennessee. Circa 1960s.

Memphis, Tennessee. Circa 1960s.

Memphis, Tennessee. Circa 1960s.

Kingston, Tennessee. Circa 1960s.

Kingston, Tennessee. Circa 1960s.

Center Street, Kingsport, Tennessee. Circa 1960s.

Highway 61, Memphis, Tennessee. Circa 1950s.

The Atlantic Refining Company was another product of the Standard dissolution. It was restricted to Pennsylvania and Delaware where it had the right to use the Standard brand. Later, Atlantic began expanding into New England and south through Virginia, the Carolinas, Georgia, and Florida under the Atlantic brand.

Sinclair was founded in 1916 in New York by Harry Sinclair. Sinclair developed an extensive chain of gasoline stations from the East Coast to the Midwest. In 1932, Sinclair merged with both the Prairie Oil and Gas Company and the Prairie Pipe Line company to form the Consolidated Oil Corporation. It continued to market under the Sinclair brand.

In 1965, Atlantic and Richfield merged to form Atlantic-Richfield (later changed to ARCO). At the time, Atlantic had some 8,300 stations and Richfield had over 4,400 stations. This merger gave Atlantic-Richfield a strong presence on both the East and West Coasts. In 1969, ARCO purchased Sinclair, which added another 22,000 stations to the company. In 1973, 4,500 Atlantic and Sinclair stations in eleven northeastern states (along with various terminals, bulk plants, and refineries) were sold to British Petroleum (BP) to avoid antitrust litigation. With the Department of Justice still in active pursuit, over 9,700 Sinclair stations were eventually sold to BP. ARCO agreed to keep the Sinclair brand on former Sinclair stations in twenty-one Central states. Still not satisfied, the Department of Justice forced the sale of all Sinclair stations in fourteen mid-continent states. A new Sinclair Oil Company rose out of this action.

Top Right:
7th & Chelsea, Memphis, Tennessee. Circa 1940s.

Right:
Cairo, Georgia. Circa 1930s.

Crossville, Tennessee. Circa 1930s.

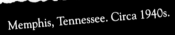

Memphis, Tennessee. Circa 1940s.

Cairo, Georgia. Circa 1950s.

Ernest Flohe's Briar Oaks Restaurant with
Sinclair pump. (Chip Flohe's Grandfather).
Briarcliff, New York. Circa 1936.

Oak Ridge Turnpike, Knoxville, Tennessee. Circa 1950s.

Roan & King, Johnson City, Tennessee. Circa 1950s.

Knoxville, Tennessee. Circa 1950s.

Jonesboro, Tennessee. Circa 1950s.

Memphis, Tennessee. Circa 1960s.

Fort Henry Drive, Kingsport, Tennessee. March 1961.

Elizabethton, Tennessee. Circa 1960s.

Knoxville, Tennessee. Circa 1960s.

Louisville, Kentucky. Circa 1960s.

Chelsea & Ash, Memphis, Tennessee. Circa 1950s.

Church Hill, Tennessee. Circa 1950s.

Memphis, Tennessee. Circa 1960s.

Clinton Highway, Knoxville,
Tennessee. Circa 1950s.

Springfield, Tennessee. Circa 1950s.

Chapman Highway, Knoxville, Tennessee. Circa 1940s.

Springfield, Tennessee. Circa 1950s.

State Street, Bristol, Tennessee. Circa 1950s.

Chapman Highway, Knoxville, Tennessee. Circa 1940s.

West Center, Kingsport, Tennessee. May 1960.

Colonial Heights, Tennessee. Circa 1966.

Memphis, Tennessee. May 1965.

Memphis, Tennessee. Circa 1960s.

CHAPTER 7:

The Gulf Oil Company began in 1901 with the discovery of the Spindletop Field of Texas. Gulf was financed and controlled by Andrew Mellon of Pittsburgh. Early on, Gulf predominately occupied West Texas. As we mentioned in Chapter 1, Gulf has claim to the first architect-designed service station in Pittsburgh in 1913. In the 1930s, Gulf extended its marketing territory into the Southeast, the Midwest, and the Northeast. By 1970, Gulf had expanded westward and was marketing in all forty-eight contiguous states.

Due to serious financial troubles, Gulf merged with Chevron (formerly Standard Oil of California) in 1984. This merger changed the face of Gulf stations across the U.S. Over 5,600 Gulf stations in the Southeast were sold to BP. Chevron converted some 2,700 Gulf stations in Texas, Louisiana, Arkansas, and Oklahoma. Today, the only branded Gulf stations in the U.S. are found in the Northeast. These stations were sold to convenience store operator, Cumberland Farms, and were allowed to keep the Gulf brand name.

Springfield, Tennessee. Circa 1950s.

Knoxville, Tennessee. Circa 1940s.

McCalla & Ben Hur, Knoxville, Tennessee. Circa 1940s.

Johnson City, Tennessee. Circa 1940s.

Kingsport, Tennessee. Circa 1940s.

Memphis, Tennessee. December 1956.

Memphis, Tennessee. July 1957.

Memphis, Tennessee. Circa 1950s.

Broadway, Knoxville, Tennessee. Circa 1966.

Manhattan, Knoxville, Tennessee. Circa 1950s.

Memphis, Tennessee. Circa 1940s.

Nashville, Tennessee. Circa 1950s.

Taken 5/8/56

Breedlove & White, Memphis, Tennessee. May 8, 1956.

Kingsport, Tennessee. Circa 1950s.

Memphis, Tennessee. Circa 1950s.

Memphis, Tennessee. Circa 1956.

Clinton Highway,
Knoxville, Tennessee.
Circa 1950s.

Nashville, Tennessee. Circa 1950s.

Somewhere in Tennessee. Circa 1960.

Erwin, Tennessee. April 1960.

Macon & Peachtree, Memphis, Tennessee. Circa 1950s.

Chapman Highway & Childerss St., Knoxville, Tennessee. August 8, 1951.

Memphis, Tennessee. September 1954.

Memphis, Tennessee. September 1954.

7th & Chelsea, Memphis, Tennessee. Circa 1940s.

Magnolia & Cherry Sts.,
Knoxville, Tennessee.
September 17, 1937.

Somewhere in Arizona. Circa 1955.

Somewhere in Tennessee. Circa 1950s.

Morristown, Tennessee.
Circa 1950s.

Royal & Lafayette Sts., Memphis, Tennessee. February 15, 1952.

Henley St., Knoxville, Tennessee. Circa 1950s.

Madison & Academy, Clarksville, Tennessee. Circa 1940s.

Kingsport, Tennessee. Circa 1940s.

Somewhere in Tennessee. Circa 1950s.

Memphis, Tennessee. Circa 1950s.

Watauga Ave., Elizabethton, Tennessee. June 1958.

Magnolia & Randolph, Knoxville, Tennessee. August 1957.

Memphis, Tennessee. Circa 1950s.

Somewhere in Tennessee.
Circa 1950s.

Somewhere in Tennessee.
Circa 1950s.

Somewhere in Tennessee.
Circa 1940s.

Sweetwater, Tennessee.
Circa 1930s.

South Roan, Johnson City, Tennessee. Circa 1950s.

South Roan, Johnson City, Tennessee. Circa 1950s.

Belle Meade, Memphis, Tennessee. Circa 1950s.

Chapman & Childress, Knoxville, Tennessee. August 8, 1951.

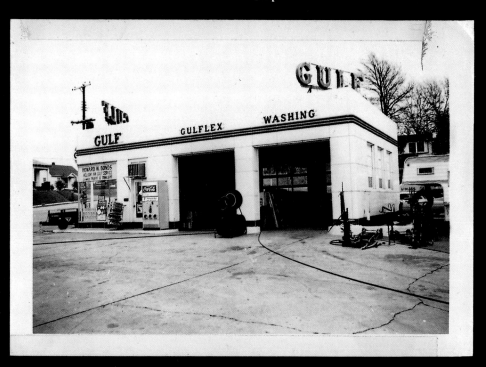

Somewhere in Tennessee. Circa 1960s.

Springfield, Tennessee. Circa 1950s.

Somewhere in Tennessee. Circa 1950s.

Somewhere in Tennessee. Circa 1950s.

Somewhere in Tennessee. Circa 1950s.

Somewhere in Tennessee. Circa 1940s.

Somewhere in Tennessee. Circa 1950s.

Knoxville, Tennessee. Circa 1950s.

Oak Ridge Turnpike, Knoxville, Tennessee. Circa 1960s.

Somewhere in Tennessee. April 1961.

Oak Ridge Turnpike, Knoxville, Tennessee. Circa 1950s.

Knoxville, Tennessee. Circa 1950s.

Knoxville, Tennessee. Circa 1950s.

Magnolia, Knoxville, Tennessee. Circa 1950s.

Knoxville, Tennessee. Circa 1960s.

Knoxville, Tennessee. July 1951.

Somewhere in Tennessee. Circa 1961.

Somewhere in Tennessee. Circa 1960s.

Somewhere in Tennessee. Circa 1940s.

Somewhere in Tennessee. Circa 1940s.

Chelsea & Payne, Memphis, Tennessee. Circa 1950s.

Somewhere in East Tennessee. Circa 1950s.

Kingsport, Tennessee. September 1962.

Kingsport, Tennessee. September 1962.

Kingsport, Tennessee. September 1962.

Center St., Kingsport, Tennessee. September 1962.

Memphis, Tennessee. September 1954.

Memphis, Tennessee. September 1954.

Memphis, Tennessee. Circa 1950s.

Sweetwater, Tennessee. Circa 1930s.

Halls, Tennessee. Circa 1960s.

Halls, Tennessee. Circa 1960s.

Halls, Tennessee. Circa 1960s.

Memphis, Tennessee. March 1957.

Top:
Memphis, Tennessee.
Circa 1950s.

Bottom Left:
Madison St.,
Clarksville, Tennessee.
Circa 1950s.

Bottom Right:
Highway 67, Butler,
Tennessee. Circa
1950s.

Raleigh,
Tennessee.
Circa 1950s.

Center St.,
Kingsport,
Tennessee.
Circa 1950s.

Highway 411,
Englewood,
Tennessee.
Circa 1930s.

Broadway & Dutch Valley, Knoxville, Tennessee. August 1951.

Memphis, Tennessee. Circa 1960s.

Memphis, Tennessee. Circa 1950s.

Watauga, Elizabethton, Tennessee. June 1958.

Highway 23, Bristol, Tennessee. Circa 1957.

Bristol, Tennessee. Circa 1957.

Main St., Elizabethton, Tennessee. Circa 1960s.

Bluff City Highway, Bristol, Tennessee. May 1959.

Route 9, Forked River, New Jersey. Circa 1920s.

Roan & Fairview, Johnson City, Tennessee. Circa 1960s.

Summer St., Greeneville, Tennessee. September 1960.

Somewhere in Tennessee. April 1961.

Memphis, Tennessee. Circa 1960s.

Memphis, Tennessee. Circa 1960s.

Broadway, Knoxville, Tennessee. March 1966.

Memphis, Tennessee. Circa 1960s.

Broadway, Knoxville, Tennessee. May 1966.

Thomas & Corrine, Memphis, Tennessee. Circa 1960s.

Summer Ave., Memphis, Tennessee. Circa 1960s.

Somewhere in Tennessee. Circa 1960s.

Somewhere in Tennessee. May 1970.

Tusculum Blvd., Greeneville, Tennessee. Circa 1960s.

Fountain City, Knoxville, Tennessee. October 1965.

Memphis, Tennessee. Circa 1960s.

Memphis, Tennessee. Circa 1960s.

Memphis, Tennessee. Circa 1960s.

Memphis, Tennessee. Circa 1960s.

Knoxville, Tennessee. January 1965.

Oak Ridge,
Tennessee.
January 1965.

Knoxville,
Tennessee.
January 1965.

Somewhere in Tennessee. Circa 1960s.

Erwin, Tennessee. Circa 1960s.

Memphis, Tennessee. Circa 1960s.

Memphis, Tennessee. Circa 1960s.

Memphis, Tennessee. Circa 1960s.

North Watkins St., Memphis,
Tennessee. Circa 1960s.

Cunningham & Trantham,
Memphis, Tennessee. Circa 1960s.

Somewhere in Tennessee. February 1970.

Memphis, Tennessee. May 1965.

Memphis, Tennessee. Circa 1960s.

Loudon, Tennessee. October 1972.

Sweetwater, Tennessee. Circa 1974.

Robertsville, Tennessee (currently Oak Ridge). Summer 1942.

CHAPTER 8:
SHELL

Royal Dutch-Shell was established in 1907 as a merger between the Shell Transport and Trading Company of Great Britain and the Royal Dutch Petroleum Company. Shell began marketing in the United States in 1912 through its marketing subsidiary, The American Gasoline Company of Seattle. This has been established as the first company to sell gasoline and motor oil exclusively.

Because Shell had always imported their product up to this point, it became increasingly difficult for them to compete with U.S. producers. This forced Shell to establish its own producing fields and refineries. In 1917, Shell purchased Roxana Petroleum in St. Louis. By 1925, Shell had almost 3,000 stations in California, Oregon, and Washington and by 1929 they were marketing in all forty-eight contiguous states.

Today, Shell remains a major player in the gasoline retail market. Currently, Shell markets in all but eleven of the continental United States.

Highway 11W, Church Hill, Tennessee. Circa 1950s.

Kingsport, Tennessee. Circa 1940s.

Kingsport, Tennessee. Circa 1940s.

Memphis, Tennessee. March 1957.

Magnolia Avenue, Knoxville, Tennessee. Circa 1940s.

Location unknown. Circa 1940s.

Location unknown. Circa 1950s.

Summer Street,
Memphis,
Tennessee.
Circa 1940s.

Memphis, Tennessee.
March 1956.

Location unknown.
Circa 1950s.

Knoxville, Tennessee.
Circa 1940s.

Sevierville, Tennessee. Circa 1950s.

Sevierville, Tennessee. Circa 1950s.

Sevierville, Tennessee. Circa 1950s.

Sevierville, Tennessee. Circa 1950s.

Sevierville, Tennessee.
Circa 1950s.

Memphis, Tennessee.
Circa 1950s.

Chapman Highway,
Knoxville, Tennessee.
Circa 1950s.

Nolensville Road, Nashville,
Tennessee. Circa 1950s.

Knoxville, Tennessee. Circa 1950s.

Springfield, Tennessee. Circa 1950s.

Oak Ridge, Tennessee. Circa 1950s.

North Cumberland, Morristown, Tennessee. Circa 1952.

Knoxville, Tennessee. Circa 1940s.

West State Street, Bristol, Tennessee. Circa 1950s.

Kingsport, Tennessee. Circa 1950s.

Memphis, Tennessee. July 1954.

Kingsport, Tennessee. Circa 1950s.

Memphis, Tennessee. March 1957.

Location unknown. Circa 1960s.

Location unknown. Circa 1950s.

Memphis, Tennessee. July 1954.

Wilcox & Lincoln, Kingsport,
Tennessee. September 1962.

Center Street, Kingsport, Tennessee. September 1962.

Kingsport, Tennessee.
September 1962.

North Cleveland, Memphis, Tennessee. Circa 1960s.

Location unknown. January 1965.

Greeneville, Tennessee. Circa 1960s.

Oak Ridge, Tennessee. Circa 1950s.

Elizabethton, Tennessee. Circa 1960s.

Memphis, Tennessee. Circa 1960s.

Memphis, Tennessee. Circa 1960s.

Knoxville, Tennessee. Circa 1960s.

Kingsport, Tennessee. September 1962.

Kingsport, Tennessee. September 1962.

Location unknown. Circa 1960s.

Location unknown. May 1961.

Knoxville, Tennessee. Circa 1960s.

Location unknown. April 1972.

Kingsport, Tennessee. September 1962.

Memphis, Tennessee. Circa 1960s.

Knoxville, Tennessee. November 1963.

Pure Oil Company traces its beginnings to Oil City, Pennsylvania, and the Producers Oil Company in 1891. In 1895, Producers changed their name to Pure. Pure began gasoline marketing in 1914, but was mainly involved with public utilities (much like Cities Service).

Beginning in the 1920s, Pure began to grow its gasoline business through acquisitions. One of these acquisitions was the Wofford Oil Companies of Georgia and Alabama in 1925.

Wofford had marketed Woco-Pep, which was a benzol blended gasoline. Pure continued to market Woco-Pep throughout the South until World War II. By the late 1930s, Pure Oil supplied products to over 17,000 branded jobbers. Pure and Union Oil (Unocal) merged in 1965. This merger created a chain of over 20,000 retail outlets. Today, Unocal has trimmed back to a little over 7,400 outlets located throughout the Eastern and Western United States.

Left:
Elizabethton, Tennessee. Circa 1950s.

Below:
North Roan Street, Johnson City, Tennessee. Circa 1950s.

Kingsport, Tennessee. Circa 1940s.

Vienna, Georgia. Circa 1940s.

Vienna, Georgia. Circa 1950s.

Knoxville, Tennessee. Circa 1950s.

Hollywood Avenue, Memphis, Tennessee. Circa 1950s.

Elizabethton, Tennessee. Circa 1960s.

Hollywood Avenue, Memphis, Tennessee. Circa 1950s.

Bristol, Tennessee. Circa 1950s.

Morristown, Tennessee. Circa 1950s.

Memphis, Tennessee. Circa 1950s.

Knoxville, Tennessee. Circa 1950s.

Memphis, Tennessee. Circa 1950s.

Knoxville, Tennessee. Circa 1950s.

West State Street, Bristol, Tennessee. Circa 1950s.

Magnolia Avenue, Knoxville, Tennessee. Circa 1950s.

Erwin, Tennessee.
Circa 1950s.

Memphis, Tennessee. Circa 1950s.

Location unknown. Circa 1940s.

Memphis, Tennessee. Circa 1950s

Memphis, Tennessee. Circa 1960s.

Far Left:
Summer Avenue,
Memphis, Tennessee.
Circa 1960s.

Left:
Winchester,
Tennessee. Circa
1960s.

Far Left:
Knoxville, Tennessee.
Circa 1960s.

Left:
Knoxville, Tennessee.
Circa 1950s.

Far Left:
Location unknown.
Circa 1960s.

Left:
Location unknown.
Circa 1970s.

Oak Ridge Highway, Knoxville, Tennessee. Circa 1950s.

Knoxville, Tennessee. Circa 1950s.

Summer Avenue, Memphis, Tennessee. Circa 1960s.

Memphis, Tennessee. Circa 1960s.

Similar to Gulf, Texaco originated in Port Arthur, Texas, in 1902 as a result of the Spindletop Field. Texaco began as an aggressive producer, refiner, and marketer. Like so many other companies, Texaco grew by buying others. As they expanded, they bought Galena-Signal Oil Company, the California Petroleum Company, the Indian Oil Refining Company (originator of Havoline brand motor oil), the Paragon Oil Company, and eventually, the Getty Oil Company (Tydol, Skelly, and Associated). Texaco was forced by the Department of Justice to dispose of many of the former Getty stations. An independent Getty still operates from Maine to Virginia.

Texaco became the first oil company to operate in all forty-eight (eventually all fifty) states and is perhaps the most popular gasoline station many Americans remember. In 1932, Texaco introduced their Fire Chief brand gasoline and began their nationwide radio advertising campaign. Through the years, their advertising has included such popular spokesmen as Milton Berle and Bob Hope. Texaco has always appealed to children in their advertising. Evidence of this is the number of Texaco toys sold and given away through the years (the North Dakota Tanker, Fire Chief Hat, numerous toy metal trucks, etc.).

Currently, Texaco has over 15,000 outlets in forty-four states (almost 3,000 in Texas alone).

Previous Page:
Airplane station, Clinton Highway, Knoxville, Tennessee. Circa 1930s.

Location unknown. Circa 1930s.

Cairo, Georgia. Circa 1910.

Dickerson Road, Nashville, Tennessee. Circa 1940s.

Location unknown. Circa 1930s.

Rare nighttime photo. Shafer's Station, Clinton Highway, Knoxville, Tennessee. Circa 1950s.

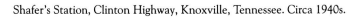

Shafer's Station, Clinton Highway, Knoxville, Tennessee. Circa 1940s.

Shafer's Station, Clinton Highway, Knoxville, Tennessee. Circa 1940s.

Shafer's Station, Clinton Highway, Knoxville, Tennessee. Circa 1950s.

Oak Ridge Highway, Knoxville, Tennessee. Circa 1950s.

Memphis, Tennessee. Circa 1940s.

Memphis, Tennessee. Circa 1950s.

Central Avenue, Memphis,
Tennessee. Circa 1950s.

Bluff City Highway,
near Bristol,
Tennessee. Circa 1959.

Nolensville Road, Nashville,
Tennessee. Circa 1950s.

East Main Street, Gallatin,
Tennessee. Circa 1950s.

Memphis, Tennessee. September 1957.

English, Indiana. Circa 1950s.

Poplar Avenue, Memphis, Tennessee. March 1956.

Elizabethton, Tennessee. Circa 1950s.

Somewhere in Mississippi. Circa 1950s.

Broadway and Cedar Avenue,
Knoxville, Tennessee. March 1966.

Evergreen
Street,
Memphis,
Tennessee.
Circa 1950s.

South Third,
Memphis,
Tennessee.
Circa 1960s.

South Third, Memphis,
Tennessee. March 1957.

Clinton Highway, Knoxville,
Tennessee. Circa 1950s.

Henley and Cumberland,
Knoxville, Tennessee.
Circa 1950s.

Georgetown Texaco, Memphis, Tennessee. March 1956.

Summer Avenue, Memphis, Tennessee. Circa 1960s.

Location unknown. April 1961.

Sevierville, Tennessee. Circa 1965.

Top:
Broadway at 5 Points, Maryville, Tennessee. Circa 1956.

BelowLeft:
Springfield, Tennessee. Circa 1950s.

Below Right:
North Cumberland, Morristown, Tennessee. Circa 1964.

Bottom Left:
Oak Ridge Turnpike, Oak Ridge, Tennessee. Circa 1950s.

Bottom Right:
Knoxville, Tennessee. Circa 1950s.

Knoxville, Tennessee. Circa 1950s.

Memphis, Tennessee. Circa 1950s.

Memphis, Tennessee. Circa 1950s.

Knoxville, Tennessee. Circa 1950s.

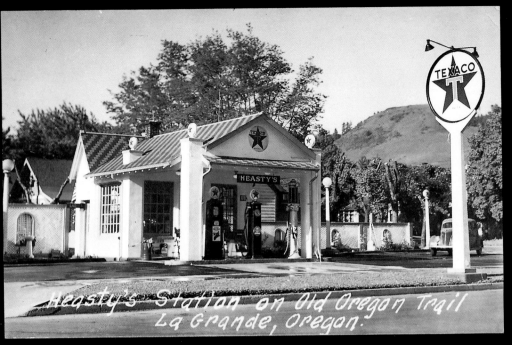

LaGrange, Oregon. Circa 1940s.

Chapman Highway, Knoxville,
Tennessee. Circa 1940s.

Knoxville, Tennessee. Circa 1950s.

Hernando, Mississippi. July 1962.

West Center Street, Kingsport, Tennessee. September 1962.

Memphis, Tennessee. Circa 1950s.

Memphis, Tennessee. Circa 1950s.

Dickerson Road, Nashville, Tennessee. Circa 1940s.

Church Hill, Tennessee. Circa 1950s.

Elizabethton, Tennessee. Circa 1960s.

Bristol, Tennessee. Circa 1957.

Location unknown. Circa 1950s.

Somewhere in Mississippi. Circa 1950s.

Memphis, Tennessee. Circa 1950s.

West Center Street, Kingsport, Tennessee. Circa 1940s.

Clinton Highway, Knoxville, Tennessee. Circa 1950s.

Memphis, Tennessee. May 1965.

Location unknown. May 1970.

Louisville, Kentucky. Circa 1970s.

Doyle, Tennessee. Circa 1920s.

Site Oil Company is a mid-West discount retailer located in Clayton, Missouri. They operated under the Cresyl brand in the 1930s and 1940s and switched to the Site brand after World War II.

Peoples Oil Company was a mid-South discount retailer located in Nashville. Peoples was purchased by Kerr McGee and most of the Peoples stations were rebranded Kerr McGee by 1980.

Dixie was founded in Ann Arbor, Michigan, in 1926 as a distributor organization of discount retailers. Dixie saw great expansion until the gasoline shortages of World War II forced many of its agents out of business. A limited number of Dixie stations still operate today.

Bay Petroleum was founded in McPherson, Kansas, in the late 1930s. In 1961, Tennessee Bay merged with Tennessee Gas Transmission to form Tenneco and moved its headquarters to Houston, Texas. When Tenneco decided to get out of retail marketing, it sold its Bay branded stations to Dixie Oil of Tifton, Georgia. Dixie began in 1947 and is the only retailer who currently uses globes. There are several independent Bay stations that are currently operated by Dixie (mostly in Georgia and Florida).

Nunis was a Memphis-based independent.

Pride Oil Company is based in Knoxville, Tennessee. Pride has operated in East Tennessee since the late 1940s and is currently a Phillips 66 jobber.

Red Ace Petroleum was an independent based in Nashville, Tennessee. They were bought by Mapco in the 1970s.

Consumers Oil Company was an independent based in Nashville, Tennessee.

The Fleet brand belonged to Shelby Petroleum of La Follette, Tennessee. The stations were rebranded from Fleet to Peer around 1960.

Central Avenue, Memphis, Tennessee. Circa 1960s.

Top Left:
Central Avenue, Memphis, Tennessee. Circa 1960s.

Top Right:
Chapman Highway, Knoxville, Tennessee. Circa 1940s.

Bottom Left:
Bluff City, Tennessee. June 1959.

Bottom Right:
Kingsport, Tennessee. March 1961.

155

Knoxville, Tennessee. December 1964.

Albany, Georgia. Circa 1960s.

LaGrange, Georgia. Circa 1960s.

Memphis, Tennessee. Circa 1960s.

Oak Ridge, Tennessee. Circa 1960s.

Kingsport, Tennessee. September 1962.

Winchester, Tennessee. September 1964.

North Cumberland, Morristown, Tennessee. Circa 1960s.

Winchester, Tennessee. Circa 1960s.

Knoxville, Tennessee. Circa 1960s.

SUGGESTED READING

Books

Benjamin, Scott and Wayne Henderson. *Gas Stations: Landmarks of the American Roadside*. Osceola, WI: Motorbooks International, 1995.

_____. *Standard Oil: The First 125 Years*. Osceola, WI: Motorbooks International, 1995.

Helms, Todd P. *The Conoco Collector's Bible*. Atglen, PA: Schiffer Publishing Ltd., 1995.

Jakle, John A. and Keith A. Sculle. *The Gas Station in America*. Baltimore: The John Hopkins University Press, 1994.

Kirn, M., ed. *American Service Stations 1935-43*. Minneapolis, MN: Iconografix, 1995.

Witzel, Michael Karl. *The American Gas Station: History and Folklore of the Gas Station in American Car Culture*. Osceola, WI: Motorbooks International, 1992.

_____. *Gas Station Memories*. Osceola, WI: Motorbooks International, 1994.

Magazines

"Check the Oil!", P.O. Box 937, Powell, OH 43065-0937.

Mobilia, P.O. Box 575, Middlebury, VT 05753.

Petroleum Collectibles Monthly, 411 Forest St., LaGrange, OH 44050.

Tiger Hitest Magazine, P.O. Box 1651, Broken Arrow, OK 74013.